Thr Dollars

and

Three Suitcases

What's Next?

DWAYNE M. THOMAS

ISBN 979-8-89043-736-5 (paperback)
ISBN 979-8-89043-737-2 (digital)

Christian Faith Publishing
832 Park Avenue
Meadville, PA 16335
www.christianfaithpublishing.com

Printed in the United States of America

Now unto the King eternal, immortal, invisible, the only wise God, be honour and glory for ever and ever. Amen.

—KJV

I want to dedicate this book to my wife, Andrea; my daughter, Essence; and my parents, David and Celeste Thomas.

Jude 1:24 reminds me of this:

> Now unto him that is able
> to keep you from "falling," and
> to present you faultless before the
> presence of his glory with exceed-
> ing joy.

(This is my testimony.)

My journey started on July 1, 1985, in Bakersfield, California. The weather was a tad above 99 percent. To me, it was considered an extreme heat wave on that special day with joy in my heart. Flying in from New Haven, Connecticut, my hometown living off the East Coast of the temperature of the normal 70–80 percent was a major change of a different climate that I had to embrace.

I left behind my divorced parents, siblings, extended family, a few friends, and some acquaintances whom I knew to start my new life at the very young age of twenty-three. I needed more sense of direction from God, who was the driver at that moment in time. There were mixed emotions from them—happy, sad, doubtful; others mocked and laughed with disbelief, but I was determined to see it through.

It was burning in my heart early as a child to move to California one day. In grade school, it was my favorite state on the multicolor map in the classroom that was on canvas that you could see in the front of the class—I knew one day that could be my home. God used my mother to unselfishly release me into my destiny despite her being permanently bedridden, which had been about twenty years at that time. Others would say that I was selfish following this gravity across the whole United States county, but I couldn't shake it.

My father was in his twenties with three children: two boys and a girl. He made up his mind to raise his children on his own, by the grace of God, and he completed his task working for the US Postal Service for many years. I grew up in the projects in Church Street South in New Haven, Connecticut. My brother was about seven, I was four, and my sister was only weeks old when my mother got sick on Edgar Street in New Haven, Connecticut. In July 1985, I had to leave my mother with my family to continue the love for her like they always did while I started my journey. She needed 24-7 care in the convalescent home and to be fed, clothed, and bathed as needed. No one could really fully understand my and my sibling's pain of seeing my mother live and die in that same state until she passed away on December 18, 2013, at the age of seventy-five, and she went home to be with the Lord.

I never remember the sound of her voice and was too young to recall her tone or pitch to this very day, which was very heartbreaking. With all these traumatic changes in my life, now a new breaking was about to begin in my young adult life with God. Experiencing both worlds from each side of my family was positive and negative in life, but I was determined to find my place with God on a deeper level. I suffered from my own insecurities and personal voids in life. I needed completeness that only a sovereign God could give. When I arrived in California, after many years of seeing them, my family met me at the airport, and finally, I saw them there waving me down to get into the car. There I stood, amazed in my new beginning with *three-hundred dollars and three suitcases, asking the Lord, "What's next?"*

Chapter 1

The Wilderness Begins

I t had only been a few weeks, and I began to learn about the city of Bakersfield, California; there I stayed in my new surroundings, amazed by the beautiful homes and the sunny skies. I was impressed with the changes that awaited me. I immediately started looking for work and found myself working at Mercy Hospital in the laundry department. Long story short, it was a tough job, and I only lasted a few weeks. I was sad but glad that I was gone. My supervisor's mother was mean just like an angry bulldog. Everyone was afraid of her, and she didn't care about me, so it was all good that I was gone.

Before that happened, I got into some trouble shortly after getting the job. The temptation to explore beyond what I knew better was on my mind telling me, *I'm grown, and this is what I want to do.* Oh, how wrong I was. So therefore, it was time for me to leave. Hurt by my bad choices, it was best for me to leave my family's home. God favored me with a woman who was like an older sister at the hospital. She asked her mother if I could stay in a spare room in their second home. Her mother allowed me to eat there daily and wash my clothes as needed. This would be my first boarding home, living on my own. "I was in the hood."

Within a matter of days, I found a part-time dishwashing job at a Christian-owned family restaurant in downtown Bakersfield. They graciously allowed me to eat my lunch there for free every day. (That was how I survived a meal that I couldn't afford.) How could I ever forget Potato Shed. They sold gigantic potatoes with a variety of hot and cold toppings and sandwiches as well. I didn't make much money, and the wage was about $3.35 an hour, so I needed another job with more pay.

Jobs were not lucrative, and my skills were only high school level and prior military for serving three years in the army. So I picked up another job which was part-time at a store called Thrifty. There I served ice cream and stocked shelves. By the time

I paid my bills, I still didn't have money to buy a lot of food. Having less than $20 at times to buy two weeks' worth of groceries was not my plan to come to California, but I didn't really tell my family or friends back East for concerns of comments or negative feedback, and I was determined to make it. All that I could buy was a loaf of bread, a lot of top ramen, Kool-Aid, and maybe two pieces of meat. Where was all this going?

My transportation was the bus when I had some money, or I would just walk everywhere I needed to go. I didn't know anyone in the city but the people I stayed with. Eventually, I bought myself a nice bike, and that was how I got around, but foolishly one day, I left it outside where I lived and did not lock it up. Someone stole it in a matter of minutes. Though it was a hard lesson I learned, I was very disappointed, and I was determined not to give up hope.

I was earning better with my second job, and I decided to enroll in Bakersfield Community College to learn the piano and to keep me busy while attending church. I found out about this church one day while riding a bus. The driver was listening to a preaching message. I could not recall the title, but I knew in my spirit that I had to find this church. I would never forget this pastor. He and his family loved the Lord, and I knew that was where I needed to be. The Word of God was ministered there with power and authority, and I knew that my life needed to be more rooted and grounded with Christ, and my commitment to him needed much more adjustment and fine-tuning from the Holy Spirit.

While attending there, I made some friends and shortly got involved with the choir and other aspects of the ministry. *This was the church where I really learned about worship and praise music conducted by the music director; I will never forget how he taught me about worship music, singing unto the Lord, and adoring our Father, as I looked and gleaned at the awesome praise team. Though I was in the midst of this anointed atmosphere, the devil had other plans to destroy me.*

Coming from the brokenness of life and challenges of my decisions, the enemy plagued me with the challenges of drugs and alcohol and promiscuity which ran me like a wild horse, and I cried for God to pull me out of the pit of my flesh, some things my family back East knew about and others did not. I can remember many good times that we had, like barbecue parties, family outings, Christmas gatherings, Thanksgiving, and birthday celebrations, but a deep pain inside rested in my soul like an anchor, and my heart was drowning, and only God could fix it.

I went to parties and hung out almost seven days a week. These were taking a toll on my life, and *I couldn't keep running from God and not living the life that I professed during the day and was some junk at night.* As months went by, I was just flowing down the river with no direction. I will never forget the Lord spoke to me profoundly while I was taking a bath and singing in the bathroom, and he told me that he loved me. I bawled like a baby knowing what a wretched life I was playing with at times. That was when I stepped off the plane on July 1, 1985. God became my focus and my life despite my shortcomings!

I don't recall if it had been weeks or months that passed that the Lord clearly spoke again in my spirit. This time he said to me at the kitchen table while I was eating a bowl of cereal, "Prepare thyself for thy wife." *How could this be, God?*

Well, I wasn't looking really hard, but there was this sister I liked at church. She could sing, she dressed nice, and her family was well-to-do financially, but I didn't catch her eye, and besides, I only had a bike and a few nice clothes, and I didn't really have a good job at the time. At twenty-three, I could not afford a wardrobe that was trendy to really impress her, and I'd seen a guy in the church whom she took a liking to, and he drove a nice BMW, wore a nice suit, and had an excellent job, so I did not meet her required taste, so I moved on.

I spoke to one of the ministers at my church and told him what the Lord said to me and asked him what I should do, and he told me to pray and listen to God for more direction. Shortly after speaking to him, the father started the uprooting process of the issues of my heart. This is where the breaking of the fallowed ground that I needed in my life had begun. Will I listen or give in to the devil's calls in my mind, or will I run to the safety of a loving God who was waiting for his son to return back home? I was in a state of conviction of grieving the Holy Spirit, spending what little money I had on drinking and going out of town, and doing my own thing that was not in the Father's best interest for me. I had God in my heart, yet I struggled to live a holy life and to commit my lifestyle to the kingdom like we all have to do. The Bible says in Romans 3:23,

> All have sinned, and come
> short of the glory of God!

Truth be told, readers, we all have sinned…and come short of his glory, so stop raising your eyebrows.

THREE HUNDRED DOLLARS
AND THREE SUITCASES

Everyone has had bones in their closets and dirt underneath their rugs!

My point is to let him wash it out. As long as you're breathing, he's not done, if you let him heal your wounded hearts and help you find your lost mind. He knows the location!

Thoughts

Chapter 2

Let the Purging Continue

Times were getting tougher. I still couldn't get a job that paid decent money, and I didn't have a car for other opportunities further away where I could earn more. My boss at Thrifty let me go because I couldn't keep up with the union dues. I had asked to not be a part of it and receive a little less; they denied me, and that was the end of my second job. Now I was barely making ends meet.

I met a nice lady and her son at church before this had happened, and she had a spare room for boarding. She taught me a lot about handling finances and taking care of business. She was disciplined and very focused. I didn't always like her delivery, but in the end, until I moved out, I will never forget her drive and determination for herself and her son.

A new door had opened up for me, and I headed north to Sacramento on a Greyhound bus to stay with a relative until I got on my feet. He was ready and willing to give his best so that I could adjust to the new city and changes. It was so exciting, and there were many things to do compared to Bakersfield, but the dark clouds quickly covered me with worldly pleasures that stalked me. My former pastor in Bakersfield recommended a church, and I went there and started to fix the brokenness of my soul. This was a large church and well-to-do, but the enemy was busy too. I took the bait by partying, and I was on the hook again for his lies. The devil will always offer you more things that you like so that you can be sure to drown in them. He wants us dead!

> For if ye live after the flesh,
> ye shall die: but if ye through the
> Spirit do mortify the deeds of the
> body, ye shall live! (Romans 8:13)

We must mortify the deeds of our flesh, or it will drag us down the street like a dog! (We can scream and holler and throw our hands up to God, but what is hap-

pening is that we are in our process, like a junky in rehab. Where can you run to?) The devil will tell you that you're losing your mind, and your body will shake like you need a hit, but deliverance is on its way, and you got to fight with all your might. When your eye is not single, neither will your mind be, and now you're in a situation, and you don't know what to do. We say that we will never do this, but what can you say looking into the mirror of your decisions?

You may be hurt, but others are affected too. They just don't know, or do they? Grace kept me when I should have been in the obituary. You don't need to know the details, just the fact that I'm still alive and well because of Jesus Christ! As I look back over my life, he was and still is today right beside me throughout my journey in this thing called life! As I pressed on into him, my hunger to serve the Lord in spirit and truth became deeper, but the demon of hell was not giving up on taking my soul. *The old crowd said I was wasting my time as they fell more into the abyss, as I threw away my little black book of sin and stared further into the truth of God's Word.*

After switching to different jobs, I finally landed a full-time job. I was earning a little better and worked forty hours a week, so I could make it on my own now. It was time to leave my relative. He had been a great help to me as I was getting on my feet again and going through my trails. I could never repay his kindness to me, and I pray that God would bless him even more abundantly. Surprisingly, right down the street from my relative's home, the Lord gave me a favor with an apartment manager, and I needed a place. Even though I had only been at my job for about a month now, she let me move into my first apartment. Wow. I know it was God because things like this don't just happen! I finally had started my new job, and one day without looking for her, there she was. *Is this who God told me to prepare myself for when I was in Bakersfield? I'm still an unfinished product, Lord.*

Thoughts

Chapter 3

Her Name Is Andrea

I got a new job and a new environment. Life was moving forward. The old me had been cleaned and gutted, and I was growing and maturing in my walk in Christ.

This is what God had intended for all of us. The question is this: are you willing to lie still on the Father's surgery table, or are you going to tell him what and how to remove what is not right?

Then, one day, I met Andrea. She was carrying a big Black Bible and had a serious demeanor with a no-nonsense approach. To make the long story short, she was quiet, and I just was the total opposite, fun, and loud at times. Let's chop it up with good conversation. Oh no, not her. Words were few, and we talked only as needed most of the time. I wanted to talk until she was tired or impressed, but she wasn't having it, so it took me some time to get to know her.

After some time, we grew to enjoy each other's friendship, and we would visit each other at church. *She was too saved for me, and I wasn't saved enough for her. O Lord, where is this going?* Not long after that, we parted ways to different jobs and different lives and didn't see each other for a few years. The dark clouds started to return, but my mind was fixed on serving him in spirit and in truth no matter what the cost would be. Even though we started to like each other, it was not yet the right time. *The Father could allow you to meet your soulmate, but that doesn't mean that you're both mature enough to move ahead.*

We became spiritual detectives on what the other person has or doesn't have or should or should not be doing. (*Let a man first examine himself. You're not Ebony woman, and he is not the GQ man. If that is all you're looking for, then just like the grass on the hill, it will soon fade away. You need to go to the soil—the soul of the person that God has for you. Only God can rototill the ground of their life, not you.*)

About four years later, during my growth process, Andrea and I met again, but things were different this time with both of us. Wow. What a change in us!

Thoughts

Chapter 4

The Connection at the Church

I was at my new church, and while walking down the hallway, there she was again after many years—Andrea. She had a smile on her face, and she was getting ready to leave. I said, "Hey. What are you doing at my church?"

She replied, "You're church? This is my church!"

You see, we used to go to two different churches and denominations, so the Lord had to remove that wall between us so that we could be on one accord. The Bible says,

> How can two walk together
> unless they agree? (Amos 3:3)

What was God up to? There was a spark now, and things were different. We both were active in this ministry. She was an Evangelist preaching the Word and traveling throughout the state, and I was active in the choir doing solo music and busy with the men's group. God was molding us more as we were being remolded for this next big step in our lives. The question was this: Do we just like each other? Would there be a greater commitment awaiting us? Are we willing to trust each other and dump out the secrets of our hearts, or would we be playing the role as though everything in our lives is all together? What would we do? It was time to move forward, and after a few dates out with friends and family, where was this going or not? We were sitting at my kitchen table, and the conversation arose about what we are expecting to happen next with this relationship.

Though we were connected according to the same belief and understanding of the work of our personal callings, could we open our hearts to the past, present, and future for us? I told the Lord what I was looking for in a wife and reminded him if I pour out my heart for marriage, then he has to guard my mind and heart. Unfortunately, I've seen and witnessed divorce, separation, and other things on both sides of my family, and I didn't want to go on that same path. God forbid. I did not want to experience any sudden changes in the lane of this deep dive of communication that I was embarking on right now with Andrea.

As we both stared at each other and shared our deepest concerns, both of us sat at the table and cried about some tests, tribulations, and testimonies we both had. At that moment, there was no doubt that she was the one. We made our relationship official, and shortly thereafter came the engagement but not without more blows from the enemy.

Thoughts

Chapter 5

Where Did She Come From?

While pressing on to greater things, now other people had opinions about me. "He's not a preacher like you, Andrea," "Does he have a state job like you?" "Where is his car?" "Can he dress sharp like us?" and "I know that he's a worshipper, and he can sing some and can operate in the gifts of the spirit, but is that all?"

Don't let the naysayers pick you apart. Take a stand and let God do the rest, shoulders back and head forward—that is the prescription. There was no problem with me. Andrea saw my potential and pushed me in prayer and stood by my side, as I pressed on to my next level in God! (I was already confident of the Lord's work in and through me, but her moral support allowed us to stand firm on the promises of God.)

There was a short period of time that my phone was out of order temporary, and Andrea had allowed me to use her number as a backup for any new job offers. To my surprise, a young lady whom I went to lunch with offered me to use her number as well, which was an attempt to interrupt our new courtship. The enemy is always full of distractions. Beware!

(*You have to watch and pray after you say to that special one, she's the only one and no one else! Most importantly, you vow to the Lord to live a life pleasing to him and not the deeds of your flesh. The flesh is like fire. You will never satisfy it, and only God himself can stop that damming fire against your soul with his word. You got to fight the devil like it's your last breath, and that last breath is here on earth. Where will you be with that final exhale? Choose God.*

Thoughts

Chapter 6

It's Been Over Two-Plus Years of Courting; What's the Problem?

As men and women, we try to have everything picture-perfect before getting married—that means having the right job, great money, and awesome support. There is no such thing because every lacking area will be complete in each other's life at that time—good credit, bad credit, no credit, previous relationships' soul ties, and other issues. The planning time, who would be going to the wedding, whether or not you have savings to pay for this, and where you would live are the many areas of choices to bring into prayer. Sometimes the agreement is fifty-fifty; other times, it's forty-sixty. You need to talk about how important it is and strive to have a working plan. The conversation about finances must be forthright regardless of who makes more or less money. Things can get very heated offensively and defensively as the big day approaches!

Did we fuss during our courtship? We sure did, but we managed to work through it, but not without another fight with the enemy. I finally saved enough money to purchase a small engagement ring though it was tiny. Looking at it now, Andrea was proud of it! The short story was, I bought both our rings, and she left them in the boxes in her bedroom at her apartment and never moved them but only glean at them daily. One day she came home to look at them and they were stolen out of her bedroom. We found out that the maintenance man had stolen them. He accused me, but I did not live with Andrea and had my own apartment and had never stayed in her house at all. He was lying. We reported him, and shortly after, he was fired and investigated for other crimes against women in her apartment complex. The Bible says,

> No weapon that is form against you shall prosper. (Isaiah 54:17)

Don't get me wrong. It's okay to have desires on your list for mates, but keep in mind now he has to mold two people together for his glory. Only he can do it, as you grow as one heartbeat in unity and love!

(Thought: You need to be counseled.)

This is so short. It's not a chapter, but I need to say it. We went to Marriage Counseling to get direction for our new lives, and by this time, we had matured even more. Though neither of us was completed in our sight, we both had a foundation to build upon which is Jesus Christ our Lord and Savior, and the guidelines from our overseer. I was so nervous and wanted to know 200 percent that I wasn't moving fast and God was in control. Believe it or not, while Andrea, I, and the Pastor were praying, I started to speak in tongues, and God gave me my own interpretation. His peace settled in my heart from that day forward. It was so strong and powerful that it blew me away. *I'm not tooting my horn. The point is that God really came in mightily for me and Andrea to seal and comfort our hearts that this was his will for our lives together and not other people's crazy observations.*

Thoughts

Chapter 7

The Wedding Day Is Here; I am Now Walking in the Now...

Now faith is the substance of things hoped
for, the evidence of things not seen.
—Hebrews 11:1

A s I reflect on my life, I may not have understood
everything that God was doing, but I can truly
tell you that I know that he lives, cares for me, and
desires the very best for me according to Jeremiah
29:11:

For I know the thoughts
that I think toward you, saith the

THREE HUNDRED DOLLARS
AND THREE SUITCASES

Lord, thoughts of peace, and not
of evil, to you an expected end!

Here I stood at the front of the church with my best man waiting for my bride to walk down the aisle. I was beaming there with my royal purple and black-and-white tuxedo saying, "Lord, look what you've done after all the times that I blew it and got back up. There were many disappointments, setbacks, and times of wanting to give up, but our day is here, and you are honoring it! How can I ever repay you?"

I can't, but I can write this story of the power of God in my life. *I never claimed to be a great writer or author, but I know without a shadow of a doubt that my life has been changed... far from perfect and perfected daily through prayer, fasting, and dying daily with the help of the Holy Spirit.* How can I not mention you along with the Father and the Son? You, the Holy Spirit, have always been there for me. According to John 16:13,

> Howbeit when he, the Spirit
> of truth, is come, he will guide
> you into all truth; for he shall not
> speak of himself; but whatsoever
> he shall hear, that shall he speak;

and he will shew you things to
come.

Currently, Andrea and I will be celebrating our
twenty-eight years of marriage in August 2023. We've
pastored a church for the last ten years together and
have done outreach, visited the sick, fed the home-
less, and even taken a couple and family members in
our home to get on their feet. We sowed financially
to those who are in need, gave away clothing and nice
furniture, counseled, traveled, supported each other
in ministry, sang together, wrote songs, did studio
recordings, and worked in other parts of the body
of Christ. Though we are not perfect in any shape,
form, or fashion, we strive to live for the Lord Jesus
Christ.

The Father God has blessed us with one beautiful daughter who will be twenty-three years old
in 2023 and lives with us. We live in Olivehurst,
California, and can see the Sutter Butte mountains
during the day or night. Both of us are retired from
the state of California and are still actively doing the
work of the Lord, and our only child works at a med-
ical clinic, and we are very proud of her.

It's amazing what God will do with a made-up
mind. The question is this: what are you willing to

sacrifice to walk in the fulness of his glory, regardless of your shortcomings and the many storms that you will face? We all have them. It may not be the same as mine, but the God we serve is the same…if he is Jesus Christ the Son of the Living God! If you don't know him, I admonish you to get to know him. I would have never thought that after thirty-seven years living in California and going through my tests and trials, I would be writing a book about my life so that it may challenge you and impact your lives to hold on, not give up, and abide in the vine. You can do it.

> I am the vine, ye are the branches; He that abideth in me, and I with him, the same bringeth forth much fruit: for **without me you can do nothing!** (John 15:5)

So therefore, this is my fruit, and God has promised me more, so I guess that this won't be my only book. What do you think? So here it is, *Three Hundred Dollars and Three Suitcases: What's Next?*

Thoughts

F ather, I pray in the name of Jesus Christ that you touch every heart that reads this book. You know, God, this is a challenging task to put my life story in front of the world, but you have reminded me of your life, for my life!

Let there be a transformation in their souls and hearts and give them the mindset to surrender their will to you for your glory and not theirs.

Lord, I am but one grain of many believers across this globe, but I know that someone on this earth needs to hear this message of hope, strength, and encouragement of the Gospel of Jesus Christ.

Thank you, Father, for allowing me to live long enough to tell this story; in Jesus' name, I pray. Amen.

Your servant,
Pastor/Prophet Dwayne M. Thomas

Author's Note

I pray that you will be blessed, encouraged or challenged by my book to press on to be determined, confident, tenacious, and willing to fight for your life. How bad do you want to walk in victory through Jesus Christ?!

Please take a few moments to write a review on my different platforms where you purchased my e-book or book. Thank you for your support.

About the Author

Dwayne M. Thomas was born and raised in New Haven, Connecticut, and currently lives in Olivehurst, California. He is a third generation of the Five-Fold Ministry. He teaches and acknowledges the gifts of the spirit and operates in the office of a prophet. Dwayne accepted Christ into his life over thirty-five years ago. Dwayne and his wife have pastored Another Dimension Apostolic Ministries for ten years in the city of Sacramento and old town Elk Grove, where he has preached and taught the unadulterated Word of God by the power of the Holy Spirit. Dwayne has been ordained and licensed to share the good news of the Gospel. He has enjoyed writing this inspiring book because it has changed his life, and now it's time to pass the baton to the next generation to walk in victory and conquer the enemies. Dwayne is working on more books and will be doing some deep diving as he is led by the spirit of God. I release the anointing of God by faith in the name of Jesus to everyone who reads this book, to the one and only true living God in heaven. Amen!

For speaking engagements please contact Dwayne at etprophet99@comcast.net

Printed in the USA
CPSIA information can be obtained
at www.ICGtesting.com
JSHW021106310524
63808JS00001B/41

9 798890 437365